THE
NEW YORKER

1950-1955

ALBUM

THE
NEW YORKER
1950-1955
ALBUM

HARPER & BROTHERS · NEW YORK

Lithographed in the United States by
The Murray Printing Company, Wakefield, Mass.
Design and layout by Carmin Peppe,
of The New Yorker staff

Library of Congress Catalog Card Number: 55–8220.

"*I just can't wait to see your work, old fellow.*"

"I'm afraid this is goodbye, Miss Woodley. I've lost the battle for proxies."

1

2

3

4

"All right, now, a little smile."

5

6

"Tremaine, could I see you for a moment—alone?"

"*I'm so relieved. I was afraid they'd just touch something and it would start right up.*"

"Hey, Combs! Where the hell do you think you're going?"

"I swore they'd never take me alive, but when the time came I figured what the hell."

"Unus, duo, tres, quattuor, quinque, sex . . ."

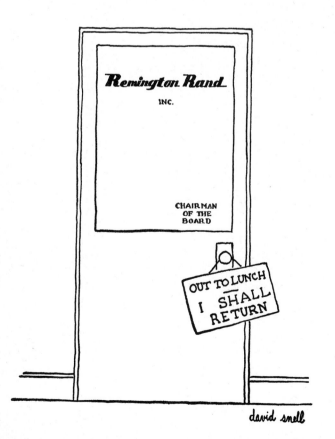

"Really, Ethel Driggs! Doesn't the Girl Scout oath we took back in Elkhart mean anything to you any more?"

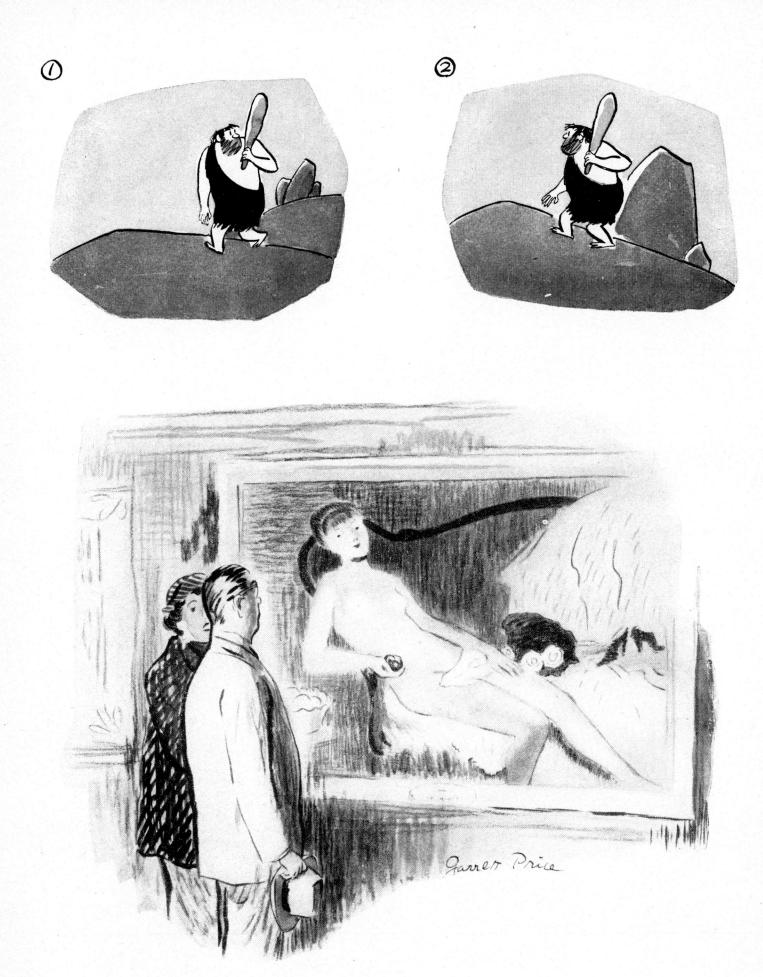

"*Mama had a sofa just like that when we lived on South Elm Street.*"

③

④

⑤

⑥

"I do think, Dr. Wurdle, that what we are witnessing here is an example of what might well be called ecological coördination."

"Now the same letter as Charles Boyer would dictate it."

"To a great human being!"

"This is the time of year when
you begin to appreciate the 'Times's' fuller coverage."

"My compliments to the chef."

"*You don't understand, Dad. It isn't the business itself—that's going great. But you can't imagine what taxes do to you today.*"

1   **2**

Dana Fradon

"At least in a movie you might be sitting next to someone."

"Now, _that's_ what I mean about Agnes."

"But we're from 'Life'!"

6

7

8

"*Watch out for him. He just had his wheels oiled.*"

"*Pardon me, sir, are you Mr. Baldwin, the patent attorney?*"

"*Now I see why everybody thinks they're extinct.*"

"*Technically nobody can touch him—but he has nothing to say.*"

"Kindly take us to your President!"

"*I am meditating.*"

"*Now, get this through your head. Edward R. Murrow is visiting me.*"

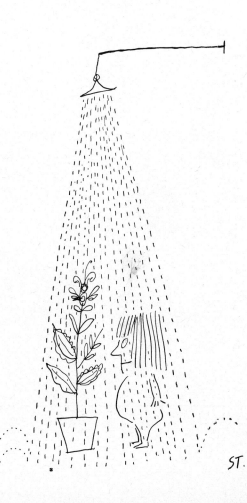

ST.

SMALL FRY

SANDLOT BASEBALL

Waiting for the signal

Fancy Dan

Slugger

"It certainly sounds good to hear English spoken again."

Circus catch

"Here it is. Take a good look at it."

Three easy outs

Rookie

Relief pitcher warming up

Butterfingers

"It's not that I don't know whether I love you or not, Herbie, it's just that I never thought of you in this connection."

"Speaking."

"This has nothing to _do_ with logic!"

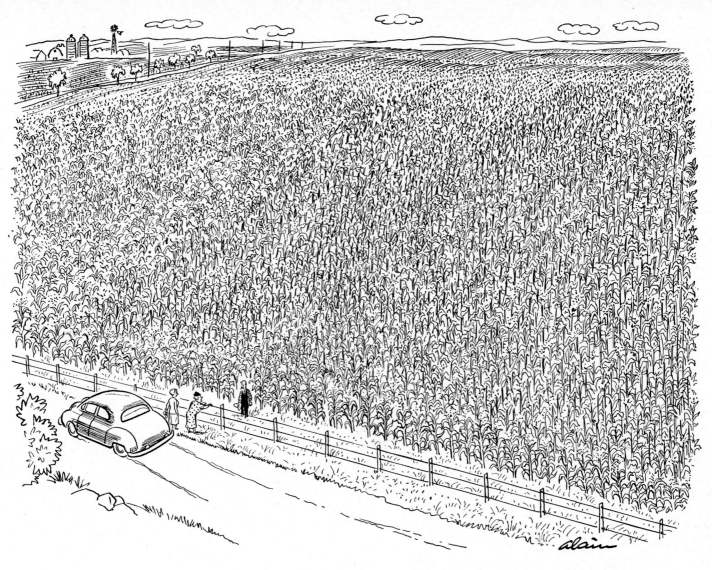

"My, you _do_ have a green thumb!"

"Damn it, Henderson, that was supposed
to be a _coffee_ break!"

"*Grab a mitt. The world situation won't deteriorate any faster
because you get in a little one o' cat.*"

"*Blast off!*"

"My goodness, Mr. Foster,
what happened to all the others?"

"His wife poisons him in the third act."

"I played on Notre Dame."

"We've already done this room. I remember that fire extinguisher."

3

4

5

6

7

8

JB Modell

"*Oh, you beautiful doll,
You great, big beautiful doll.*"

"*Now, has anyone anything else she wants to say before we start talking French?*"

"*Say, I think I see where we went off. Isn't eight times seven fifty-six?*"

"Oh, oh! I've got a hunch we're in for trouble."

"Strange—I never saw these lines before except on a catalpa leaf."

"How can I be sure you're a millionaire?"

"Martha, I can't find a damned thing!"

1

"*The makers of Siegfried beer take you to Madison Square Garden for the windup between Mike Mulvane and Rocky Rinaldo.*"

2

"*While the boys are getting set, why don't you get set—with a bottle of Siegfried . . .*"

5

"*Well, that round was in doubt. But there's no doubt about the . . .*"

6

"*. . . best beer for your money . . .*"

9

"*There's the bell ending the ninth. Time for a breather, and that means . . .*"

10

"*. . . the lager that likes you.*"

3

"...rich as velvet, smooth as silk..."

4

"Bell for the third coming up. Just time to latch onto another bottle of that beer no other beer can lay a glove on."

7

"...and while you're out there, make sure you've got enough of those blond beauties on ice."

8

"...looks like Mulvane's losing his head. You keep one on that glass of yours."

11

"Don't forget our six-can Handipak, and the money-saving case of twenty-four..."

12

"It's Rinaldo, folks, by a decision! And here's a winner by a decision, too—Siegfried beer, First for Thirst!!"

"I hope they have to do a retake. This cherry cobbler is delicious."

"Did it ever occur to you how you look to them?"

"Tonight at ten—Voice of America—
Rosemary Clooney—pass it on."

"Please don't go to any trouble. We can only stay a minute."

"Boy, I'll bet things are humming over at the 'Mirror'!"

"Many, many years ago, a little boy stood watching steam escape from his mother's samovar. 'Why not harness the steam,' he thought, 'and put it to work?' That little boy lived to invent the steam engine. His name was Alexei Petroff."

"Of course that's only an estimate. The actual cost will be somewhat more."

"The feeling is mutual, punk!"

"And so we say goodbye to beautiful New England."

"Would you prefer Mendelssohn's 'Wedding March' or 'Lohengrin'?"

"I know the type. All you'd ever get out of him would be 'We can't afford it'!"

"Why not look at it this way, Miss Paxton? Glasses, more than any other single thing, set us apart from the lower species."

"I could have bought General Motors in 1949 for twenty-six dollars a share. I could have bought Boeing for six dollars a share. I could have bought Electric Boat for thirteen dollars a share. I could have . . ."

"If I'm stupid, what about you? You married me, didn't you?"

"Well, that cleans him out."

"I say I do hear a funny noise. Why must you always stick up for the car?"

*"Gaudeamus igitur,
Juvenes dum sumus;
Post jucundam juventutem,
Post molestam senectutem
Nos habebit humus."*

"*What you really want is to marry
the girl and settle down. But you can't, because you're a gorilla.*"

"Watch it, man! The rate of exchange isn't *that* much in our favor."

"Good Lord, Gilroy, it's not for us to determine whether they're *worth* saving."

"I'm Mrs. Edward M. Barnes. Where do I live?"

"But first, our national anthem."

"They _all_ are. That's what he's in for."

"Want to know something, Dad?"

AMERICA'S PLAYGROUNDS

Shelling on Sanibel Island

"What's it matter where I've been? The important thing is I've come home to you safe and sound."

"Don't shout at me as if I were one of your armies!"

"Can I help it if we're married?"

"And why _don't_ you love me, if I might ask?"

"Do you mind if I bleach my hair?"

"<u>Now</u> who's throwing the money around?"

"...and what's more, you probably never <u>will</u> find an ad requesting intelligent companionship for an elderly millionaire."

"Who's on clavichord?"

"I suppose there's quite a story behind all this."

"Vende usted Tums?"

"*Generally speaking, your novel is quite good, but everyone here feels that the New Orleans bordello scenes lack authenticity.*"

"*I'm sure your feelings do you credit, Mrs. Carter, but you must dust this along with the others.*"

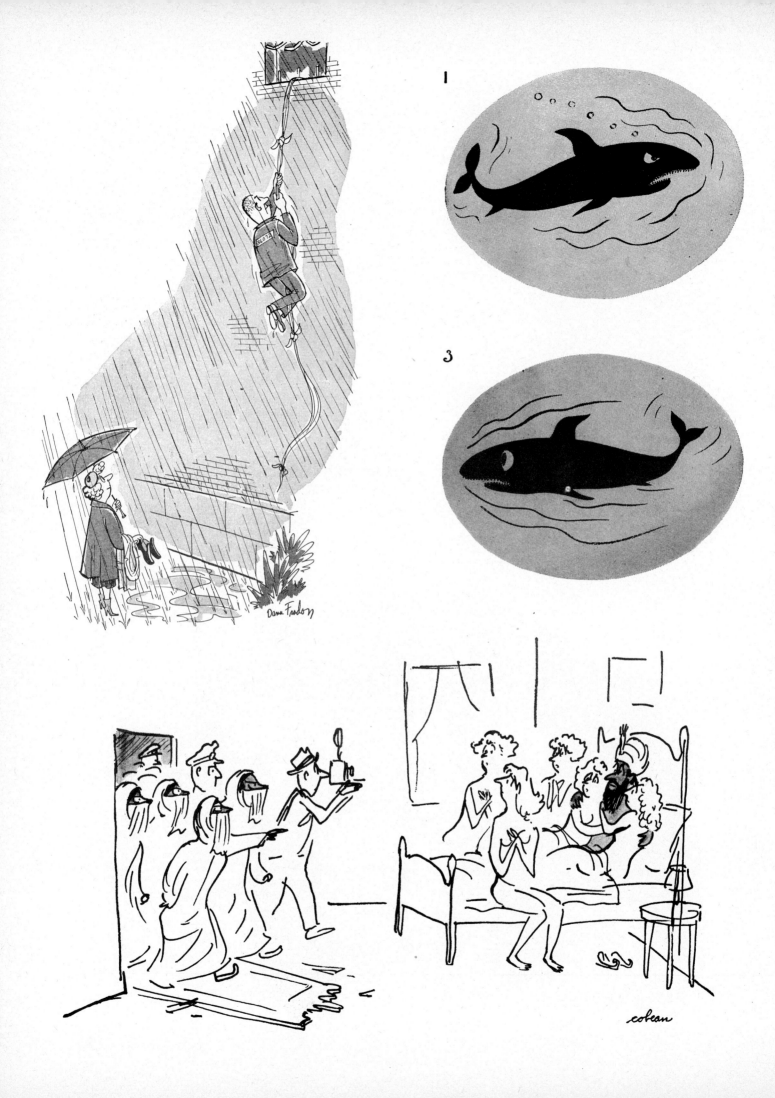

"I'm anemic."

"Mind if I play through?"

"*I'm sorry, sonny. We've run out of candy.*"

THE NEW YORKER

THE NEW YORKER

STEINBERG

"In a minute! In a minute!"

"But suppose we're not mentally superior either."

"You're fired! _You_, Preston, that is."

"My next prediction . . ."

"On rainy days, I always get this pain right through here."

"One thing I'll say for him—he's always been a good provider."

"Daddy, come at me with a knife."

"No, this isn't the Happy Time Café. This isn't the happy _anything_."

"What burns me up, I pay taxes to the Aga Khan, he gives it to Aly, Aly gives it to Rita, Rita gives it to Dick, and Dick gives it to some woman named Nora Eddington Flynn."

"Mother! Daddy's putting _two_ in his."

"I understand he didn't start selling until his later years."

"And so, in conclusion, it is with grateful hearts and a high resolve that we pledge ourselves to further those ideals you have passed on to us, to repay in some measure our debt to those who have gone before by bequeathing our best to those who will come after, to give to the future as much as we have received from the past. And now may I take advantage of this opportunity to say that, beginning next week, I will be calling on some of you about the possibility of employment."

"...Point of order ... Point of order ...
Point of order ..."

"He'll be all right, Mrs. Perkins. Keep him in bed a few
days, give him one of those pills every three hours, and
take some cooking lessons."

"Hello, Boris? Listen. Comrade Zherkov has invented something. . . . No, no, I mean really invented something!"

"I've always said two couples sharing a cottage is no good."

"Why, you swine!"

"*Please!* There happens to be a lady present."

"*The whites of your eyes are like alabaster, your pupils are like onyx, your irises like topaz, your lashes like webs of the finest gossamer . . .*"

"*One at a time! One at a time!*"

"Damn it, I __am__ looking pleasant!"

"Miss Elliott, will you bring in your notebook, the file on the Appleton merger, and a few sticks of kindling?"

"Damn it, Alice, can't you leave well enough alone!"

"Then someone yelled 'Stop, thief!' and, like a dope, I stopped."

"And stop calling me Stranger!"

"I'm afraid I haven't been much help to you, Miss. I'm awfully sorry."

CLAUDE

"How I envy you, Brother Timothy. My call didn't come till after many years wasted on the pleasures of the flesh and the so-called joys of this world."

"Your ominous silence is very effective. Don't spoil it."

"Well, *really!*"

"Good heavens, Emma! I thought _this_ was you."

Garrett Price

s. Trachtenberg.

Claude

Dana Fradon

Chon Day

"You do too have 'Harper's Bazaar'!"

"Andante! Andante!"

"I like them. They _wear_ well."

"Next time the speedometer is about to turn
over another thousand miles, maybe you'll keep quiet about it!"

"I backed up *last* time."

"Do you know what he's carrying in that briefcase?
He's carrying worries and problems and troubles,
that's what he's carrying."

"Listen, Mac. These ain't the bookstalls on the Seine!"

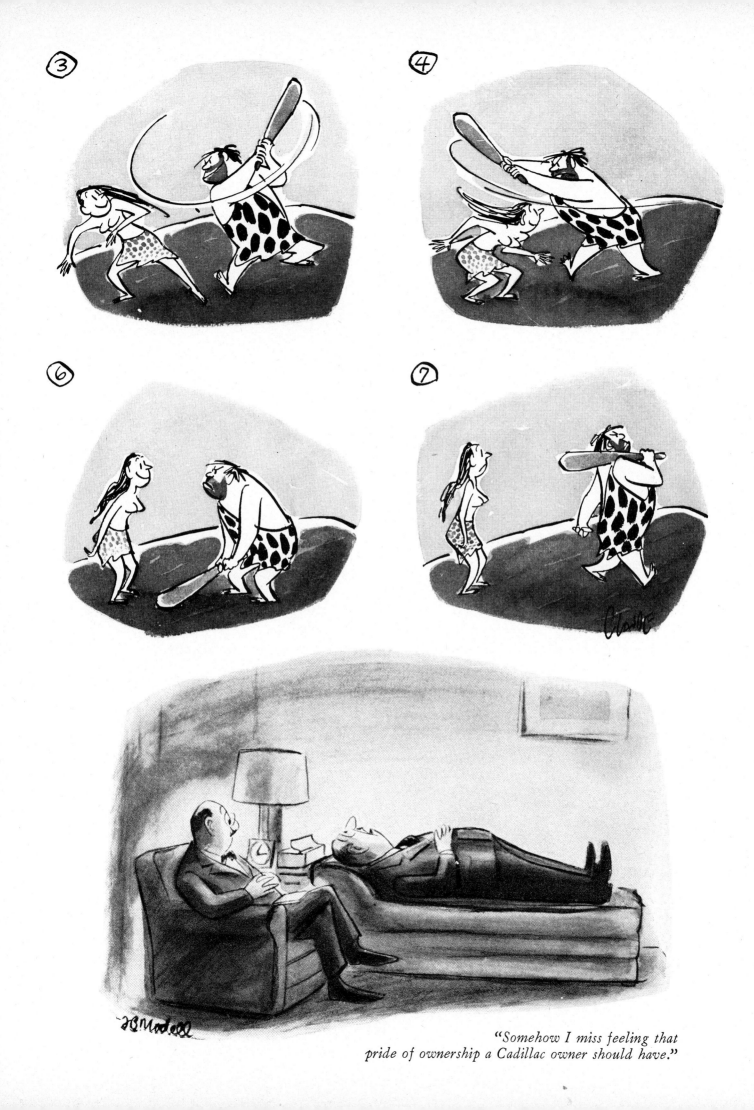

"Somehow I miss feeling that
pride of ownership a Cadillac owner should have."

"*Thank you, Madam, but I think I'd better stay out here and watch the car, and see if I can't get a good sermon on the radio.*"

"He was a great lepidopterist."

"I'd think you would have learned by now that seniority doesn't count for a thing around here."

"*By all means, dear—buy it if you really want it. We'll find the money for it somehow.*"

THE NEW YORKER

aBirnbaum

THE NEW YORKER

THE NEW YORKER

THE
NEW YORKER

"*I don't know what it is, Mr. Mardley, but there's something about this room that gives me the willies.*"

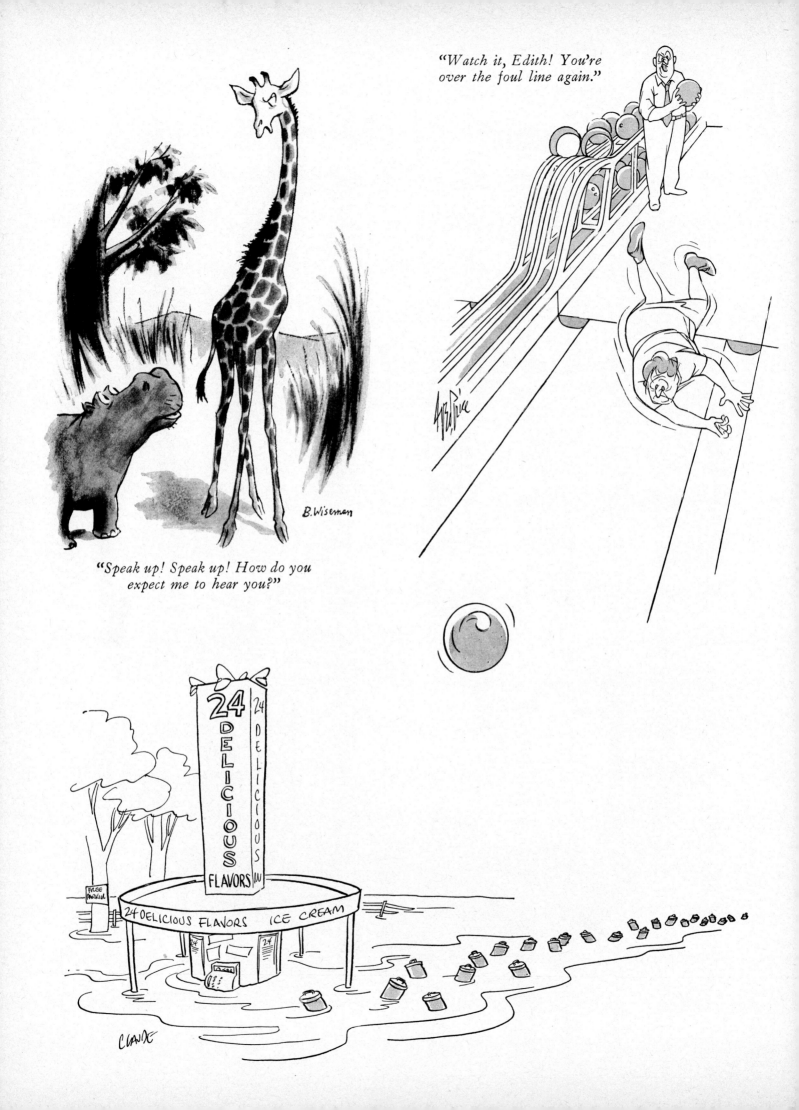

"Watch it, Edith! You're over the foul line again."

"Speak up! Speak up! How do you expect me to hear you?"

"Is it fair if I leave out the cows?"

"*I'm sorry, Mr. Hopkins, but I make it a rule never to date business associates.*"

"*I don't think it's fair to call people middle-aged just because they're not so young any more.*"

"That's the story, men. Now let's see you get out there and sell freezers."

"I think my love for Brother Valentine is less than my love for anyone else in this world."

"Thanks very much, but that wasn't me who called for help."

B. Wiseman

"Tell me, Louis, do you like your warden?"

"Frankly, the contestant sending in the most box tops stands the best chance of winning."

"*The power's off. What do we do now?*"

"*Mrs. Wallace _made_ me take them. She said they were as much ours as theirs.*"

"*I hear no complaints this morning. Am I to consider myself complimented?*"

FBModell

"I suppose I owe you a word of explanation. Less than ten seconds ago I was dropping a coin in a wishing well up in North Wilbraham, Massachusetts."

①

②

Dana Fradon

"And so, Comrades, rush right down to your local commissary and buy a box without delay."

Pedini

"As my father would have said . . ."

Whitney Darrow, Jr.

"Look, Joe, I'm calling that wind last night a terrific gale, and I don't want you crossing me up in your book."

"And don't forget the little pads, in case one of them has an idea."

"No, no, Bill! You're a commissioner now."

"I've never done any
sowing, so I really don't expect to do any reaping."

Posse

Bad hombre

Roping the maverick

"They pumped me full o' lead."

Shootin' irons handy

Complete new outfit

"Pest!"

Drawing fire

"I'm comin' in a-shootin', Black Pete!"

"Oh, Edwin, _not_ on your vacation!"

DUVAL SCHOOL OF FRENCH

IN   SORTIE

"I always feel like a damn fool when
I'm down to my last one."

1   2   3

"Why, Ted, you say the sweetest things."

LOST & FOUND

O. SOGLOW

"*I used to see your expense accounts at the office, Mr. Hofstetter,*
but gee, I never dreamed I'd be in them."

"*Carmichael, I'd like a word with you.*"

"I'll tell you later. I can't compete with that."

"And on your right, ladies and gentlemen, is Feld's Clothing Store, where you always get the most for your money."

"It may be old and threadbare, but it gets me there and brings me back."

3

4

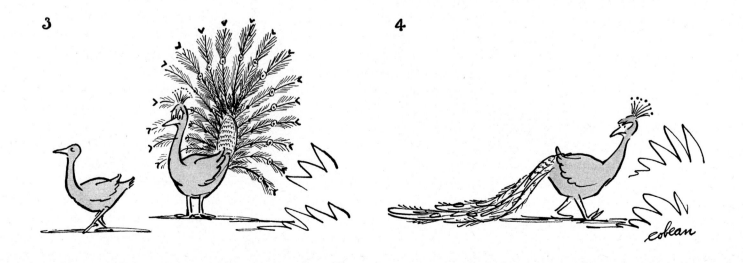

"Help! Help!"

"Do I start talking now, or do I wait until
I get on the couch?"

"At my first mention of Nietzsche, stop serving me."

"In the book, she was wearing a chartreuse taffeta with matching gloves."

"Something I can do for you, Bwana?"

"Madam, it might interest you to know that you're competing with the man who ran the fastest 220 in the Monongahela Valley Track Meet of 1928."

"*I hate everybody, regardless of race, creed, or place of national origin!*"

"And this is my secretary—Miss Foster."

CLARK

"That's just an expression, Mrs. Brown. I don't really want to take him home with me."

*"So we have to move! Am I
supposed to be in charge of the tides or something?"*

"Speaking for myself, I'd prefer aid to **trade** any day."

"When did you first discover you **were** the salt of **the** earth?"

"I did shout for help, but the tide of battle suddenly changed in my favor, thank you."

"Like I said, Professor. Moon-men; ergo, moon-women."

"How much sympathy should I give him?"

"It's a painting we've never grown tired of."

"If you'll excuse me, Madam, I should
like to make a purchase."

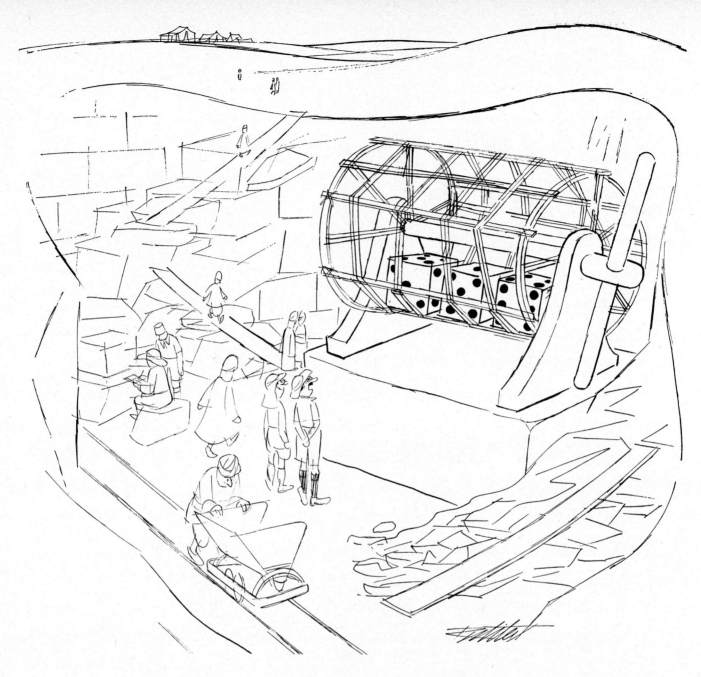

"*Well, I think we might not go too far wrong in drawing at least two conclusions about them. They were gigantic in size and addicted to gambling.*"

"*Well, I'm not striking it from* my *record!*"

"*They have a wonderful author-editor relationship.*"

"*Notice, class, how Angela circles, always keeping the desk between them . . .*"

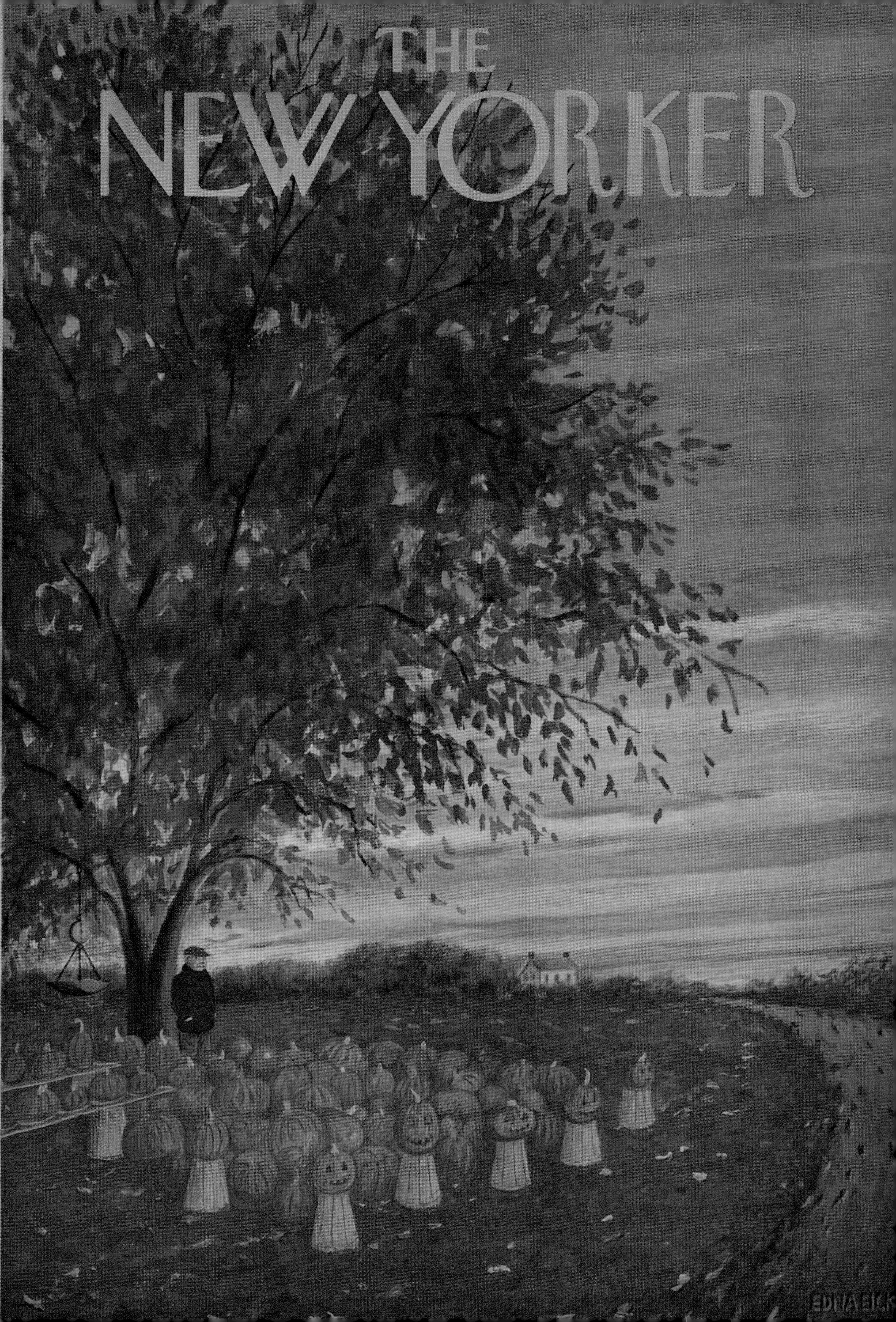
THE NEW YORKER

THE NEW YORKER

Garrett Price

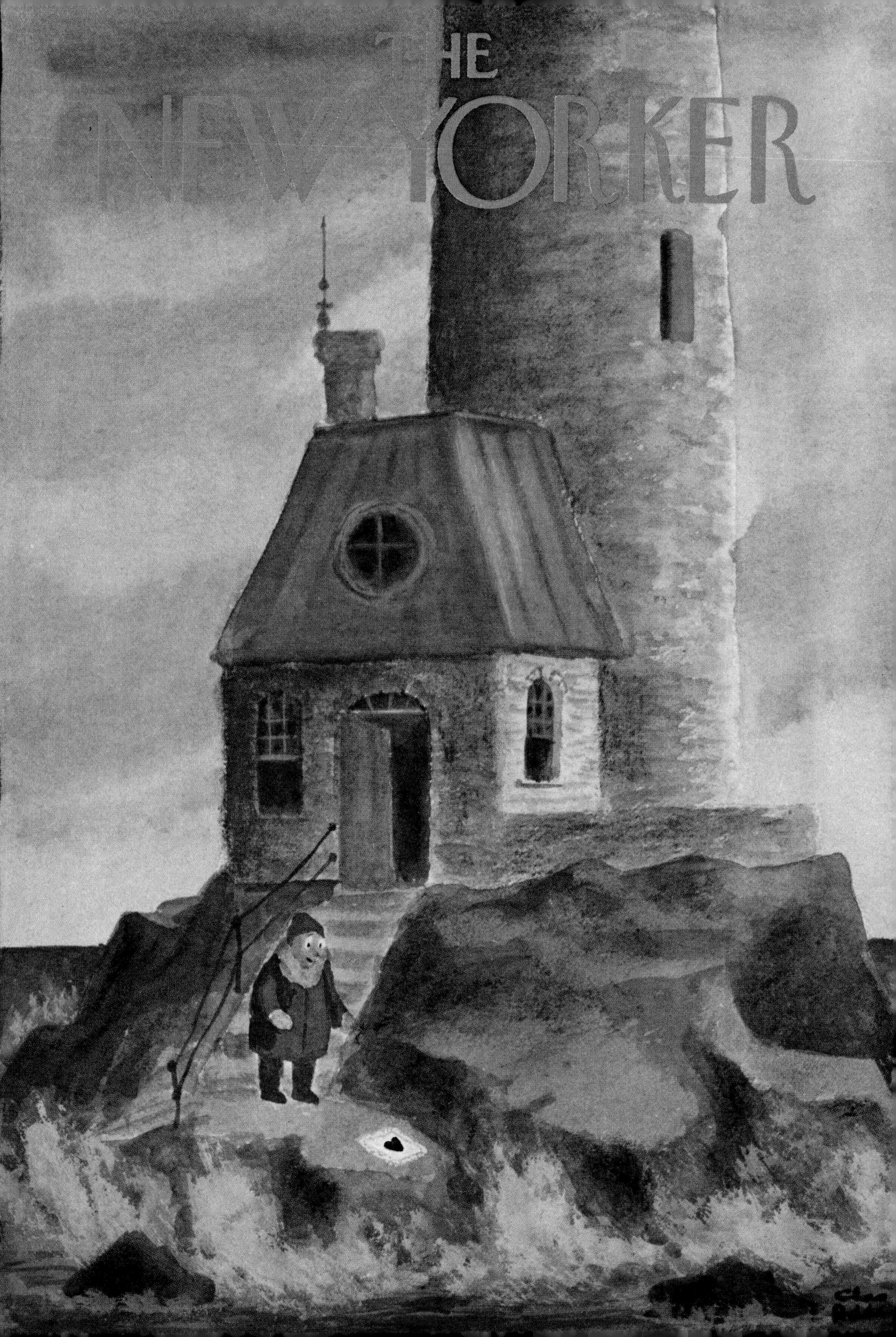
THE
NEW YORKER

THE NEW YORKER

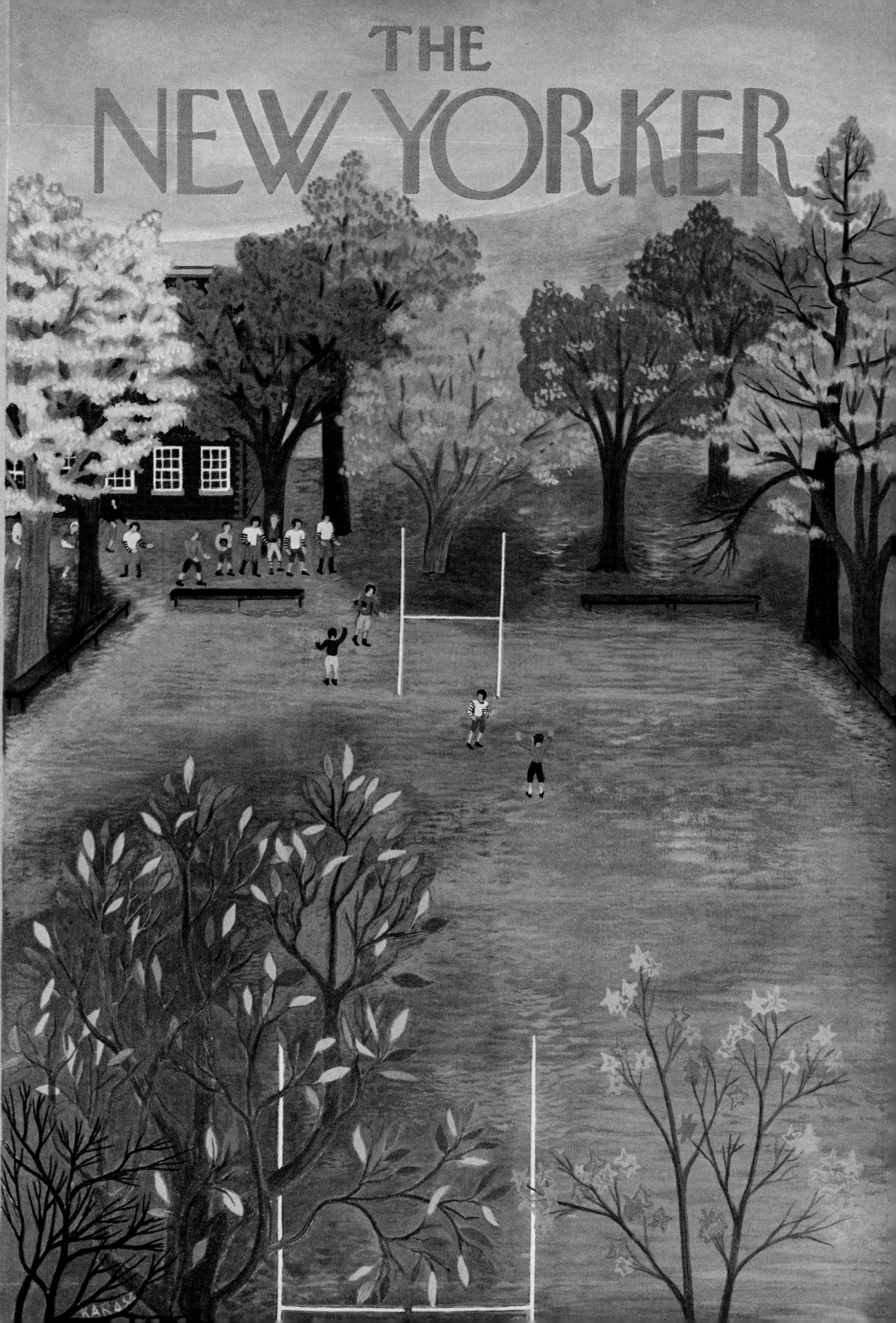
THE NEW YORKER
KARASZ

"*I really don't know if he was a Communist. We never discussed politics.*"

"*I don't listen to the evidence. I like to make up my own mind.*"

"*I think we can be congratulated on our foresight in voting ourselves these increases, thus assuring to the corporation our continuing loyal services.*"

"Whoever painted that hasn't suffered enough. Send him to Siberia."

"Something's wrong! It says my exact weight is one hundred and sixty-seven pounds and that I'm forceful in business matters, yet considerate of the feelings of others."

1

2

"Well, there's the State Department you're always crabbing about. Aren't you going to go in and give them a piece of your mind?"

"We may not be able to make 'em, but we can sure as hell cut 'em down."

"Enrich the soil with humus, which can be obtained from any nearby bog . . ."

"Yes, I knew it was loaded, but I just never <u>dreamed</u> I could hit him."

2

3

4

5

"You know damn well I take lemon!"

"*Yes, but the trouble is he always wears that mysterious smile.*"

"Well, of all the nerve!"

"My husband is tickling me."

"You're a very _stupid_ dog!"

"A gentleman across the street phoned to present his compliments and wonders if you would have dinner with him tonight."

"Hold it!"

"There we were, completely cut off, and me with one sack of flour, a case of beans, and not a single ounce of sugar."

"Death ray, fiddlesticks! Why, it doesn't even slow them up."

"Bound to happen sometime, I suppose."

"We've uncovered a whole mass of new evidence, Wilkins. Unfortunately, it proves conclusively that you're guilty."

"A motion to eat out has been made and seconded."

"*Does this by any chance refresh your memory?*"

"*Well, you don't __look__ happy.*"

"Don't you think people are stupid
to spend beautiful nights like this indoors, Miss Lamont?"

"I understand you've not only quit drinking, Bayes, but are going around telling everyone how much better you feel."

1

2

3

"Well, good night, Ahmed. If you need anything, just rub."

4

5

"Never mind about its being
only 10 P.M. in Honolulu. It's 3 A.M. here!"

"I'm a living American male. Instead of spending an entire evening sitting around
playing childish parlor games, I'd rather be home in bed. Who am I?"

"It's Oglub's boat all right, but it doesn't look like Oglub."

"Good heavens, man, your heart is breaking!"

"You hate math."

"Roll up your window, Charles. I don't want to get pneumonia with that draft blowing on the back of my neck. And for heaven's sake don't squat right in the middle of the seat and cut off my rearview mirror. And please, please stop fidgeting . . ."

"*You're trying to forget <u>one</u> woman. I'm trying to forget an entire all-girl orchestra.*"

"Me friend . . ."

"*Why, we call it—er—uh—'Old Baldy.'*"

"Oh, didn't I tell you? He's got new glasses."

"To hell with iridium! Find me a chemical that will rhyme with 'whiter' and 'brighter.'"

"Well, you can go right back to Dr. Richard T. Robbins and tell him I said your trouble is _not_ psychiatric."

"Now I've seen everything."

"It was just a small branch bank. My wife and I had simple tastes."

"Look, darling, our first bills!"

"It's all right. I just tripped on the last step."

THE NEW YORKER

Wm. Steig

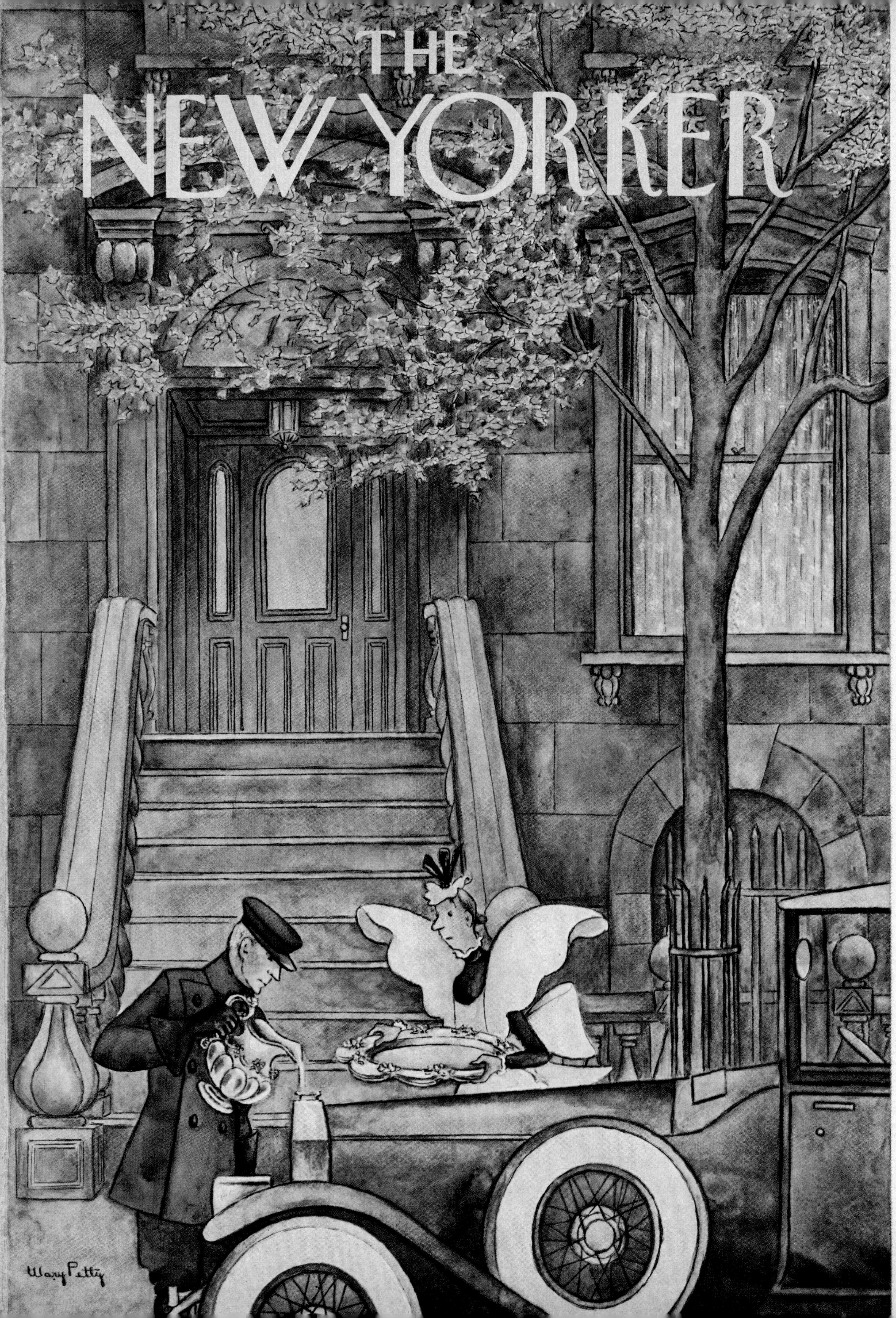
THE NEW YORKER
Mary Petty

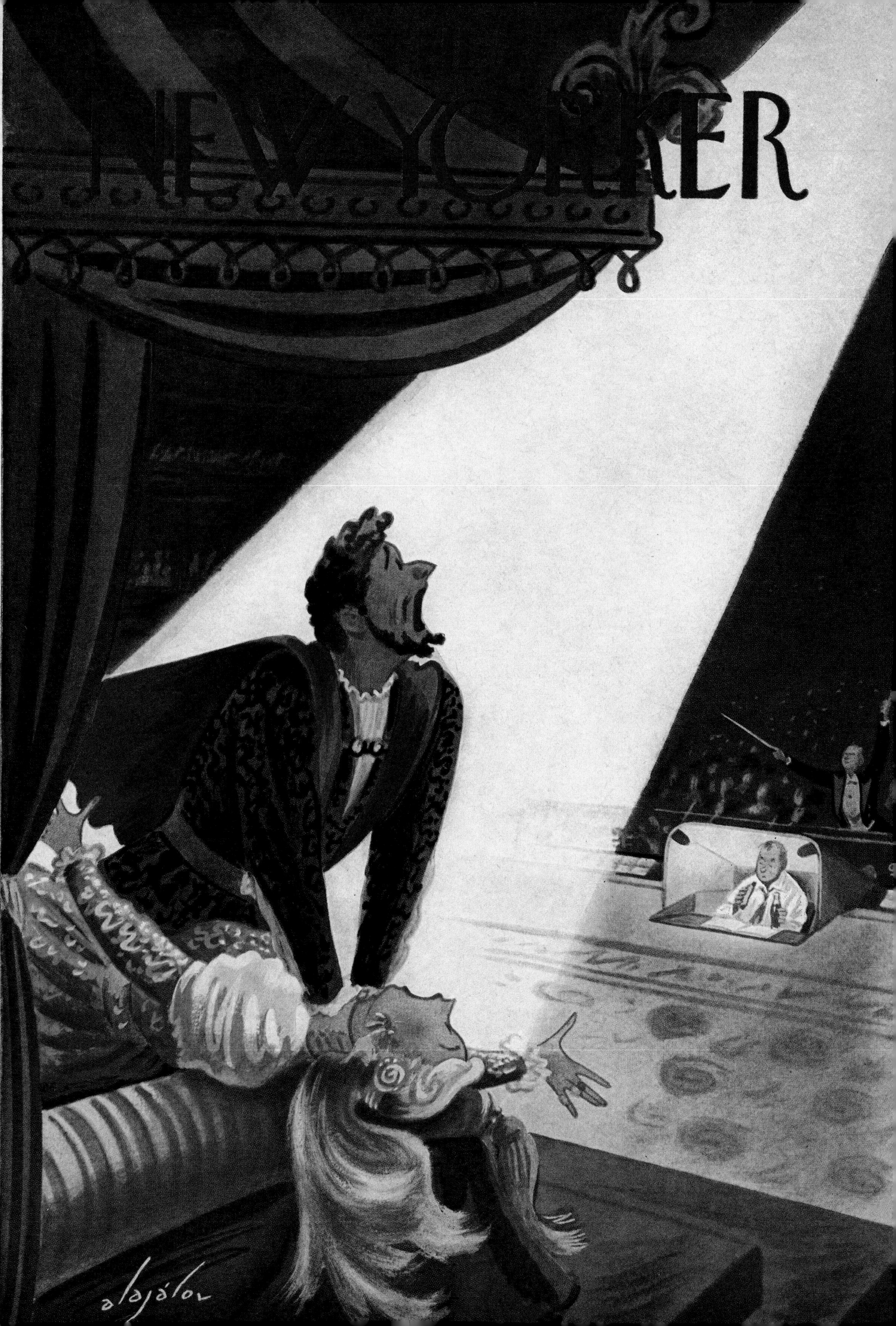
NEW YORKER
alajálov

"...way I've always dreamed of it—just you and me, a million miles from everyone. Then I ruin everything by forgetting my cigarettes."

"I've just about resigned myself to your getting twenty years."

"Aunt Claire asked you a question, dear. Are you the pitcher or the catcher?"

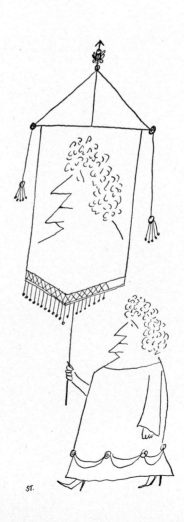

"CAN~CAN"

The lady doing a high kick in a manner popular in Montmartre in the nineties is Gwen Verdon. The other, and more restrained, girl is Lilo, an interesting importation from France. Their admirers are, respectively, Hans Conried and Peter Cookson. The show, mainly the work of Cole Porter, is at the Shubert.

"It was a nice commission. They let me eat the dove."

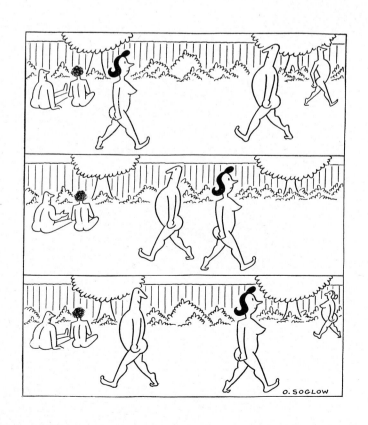

O. SOGLOW

"Ther...
have been silly of me to

ECCLESIASTICAL BOOK STORE

"DAVID and BATHSHEBA"
YOU'VE SEEN THE MOVIE
NOW READ THE BOOK

B. Wiseman

TON SMITS

"It seems mighty funny that you men always run out
of magic in an isolated spot like this."

"I wish you'd save some of that ha-ha-ha and ho-ho-ho for me."

"Now, this in no way obligates you."

"I suppose we have Mr. Young to thank for this delicious ragout?"

"...watch for stolen car, license 587J, two-door Dodge, sapphire-white
top, jewel-black hood, and heather-rose side panels."

"*If you __haven't__ been drinking, how come you're so agreeable all of a sudden?*"

"*I admire a man who has the courage of his convictions, Jenkins, but don't let me see you around here again in those damn shorts!*"

"And just what am I supposed to do with __my__ Sundays?"

"Dear Alice:

"How are you? I'm fine and getting along O.K. Today was my first day in the rock quarry. I busted up them rocks like nobody's business. You know how strong I am, Alice. The guard said he never saw a guy bust up them rocks so good the first day out . . ."

"Helen tells me you're in the Navy."

"You're kidding!"

"And now let's follow our roving camera on a surprise
visit to an average American home."

"Dad, can I have the carpet tonight?"

". . . and no one can point an accusing finger at me and say that I ever took a dollar from any man for the furtherance of my political ambitions."

"They landed in one of those new twin-engine, single-rotor Sikorsky helicopters—claim to be some sort of gods."

"Of course, with the cheaper arrow, if it falls to earth you know not where, you're only out thirty-eight cents."

"Gee, I sure hope whoever I'm going to marry isn't wasting his money or getting into bad habits."

"They landed in one of those new twin-engine, single-rotor Sikorsky helicopters—claim to be some sort of gods."

"Of course, with the cheaper arrow, if it falls to earth you know not where, you're only out thirty-eight cents."

"Gee, I sure hope whoever I'm going to marry isn't wasting his money or getting into bad habits."

"Lord, what a day!"

"Where have _you_ been? Your horse came _back_ hours ago."

"I'm sick and tired of having my evenings ruined. Why can't you ever commit one of those daring daylight robberies I keep reading about?"

"PLAIN AND FANCY"

The very plain figure in the middle of this valentine is Stefan Schnabel, and the others, beginning with the songbird in the upper left-hand corner and continuing clockwise, are Barbara Cook, Gloria Marlowe, David Daniels, Richard Derr, Nancy Andrews, Shirl Conway, and Douglas Fletcher Rodgers. They all appear in the musical about the Amish people at the Mark Hellinger.

1

2

3

4

Cem

Wm Staig

"You look so cool I could murder you."

"Slowly, steadily, the blue-coated troopers closed in for
the kill, their evil faces eager with triumph. It seemed
the end. Then suddenly from the surrounding hills there
came the welcome sound of many war whoops . . ."

"I wonder what brand _he_ smokes."

"And another thing—the ball-point pen, which cost as much as sixteen dollars when I first took office, is now available to every man, woman, and child in this state for as little as twenty-five cents."

"Sure it's a lot of money. But let's never forget one thing—it's counterfeit."

"Sleep!"

"There he goes departing from the prepared text again."

"Superb! I'll buy it."

AMERICA'S PLAYGROUNDS

St. Augustine

"*Yes, dear, I'm bowling again tonight.*"

"*He's had enough.*"

"*Imagine all that fuss over just _one_ woman!*"

"*And another feature—in case relatives should drop in unexpectedly,
this absolutely cannot be turned into a bed.*"

"*What I don't like about chess is
the way you have to sit and pretend to think!*"

"My wife gave it to me for Christmas."

*"Whatever do you see
in poor little me?"*

*"This one is dated May 10, 1934. You can
no longer go on without me."*

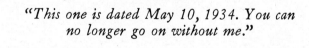

"You haven't said a pleasant word in two days!"

"There! A message of good will for all mankind."